SUPER SIMPLE

BUTTERFLY GARDENS

A KID'S GUIDE TO GARDENING

ALEX KUSKOWSKI

Super Sandcastle

An Imprint of Abdo Publishing
www.abdopublishing.com

Consulting Editor, Diane Craig,
M.A./Reading Specialist

www.abdopublishing.com

Published by Abdo Publishing, a division of ABDO, PO Box 398166, Minneapolis, Minnesota 55439. Copyright © 2015 by Abdo Consulting Group, Inc. International copyrights reserved in all countries. No part of this book may be reproduced in any form without written permission from the publisher. Super SandCastle™ is a trademark and logo of Abdo Publishing.

Printed in the United States of America, North Mankato, Minnesota
102014
012015

Editor: Liz Salzmann
Content Developer: Alex Kuskowski
Cover and Interior Design and Production: Mighty Media, Inc.
Photo Credits: Jen Schoeller, Shutterstock

The following manufacturers/names appearing in this book are trademarks:
Miracle Gro ®

Library of Congress Cataloging-in-Publication Data

Kuskowski, Alex.
  Super simple butterfly gardens : a kid's guide to gardening / Alex Kuskowski.
    pages cm. -- (Super simple gardening)
  ISBN 978-1-62403-521-0
1. Butterfly gardens--Juvenile literature. 2. Butterfly gardening--Juvenile literature. I. Title. II. Series: Kuskowski, Alex. Super simple gardening.
  QL544.6.K87 2015
  638'.5789--dc23
                    2014023604

Super SandCastle™ books are created by a team of professional educators, reading specialists, and content developers around five essential components—phonemic awareness, phonics, vocabulary, text comprehension, and fluency—to assist young readers as they develop reading skills and strategies and increase their general knowledge. All books are written, reviewed, and leveled for guided reading, early reading intervention, and Accelerated Reader® programs for use in shared, guided, and independent reading and writing activities to support a balanced approach to literacy instruction.

TO ADULT HELPERS

Gardening is a lifelong skill. It is fun and simple to learn. There are a few things to remember to keep kids safe. Gardening requires commitment. Help your children stay dedicated to watering and caring for their plants. Some activities in this book recommend adult supervision. Some use sharp tools. Be sure to review the activities before starting and be ready to assist your budding gardeners when necessary.

Key Symbols

In this book you may see these symbols. Here is what they mean.

Sharp!
You will be working with a sharp object. Get help.

Outside Light
Put your plant outside.
Direct Light = in sunlight.
Indirect Light = in shade.

TABLE OF CONTENTS

Get into Gardening 4
Butterfly Gardens 5
Plant Planning 6
Outside Gardening 7
Tools 8
Safety 9
Dig into Dirt 10
Plant Care 11
Location Station 12
Butterfly Necessities 14
Butterfly Favorites 15
Butterfly Bar 16
Fun Feeder 20
Garden in a Bag 24
Boot Planter 28
Glossary 32

GET INTO GARDENING

Dig into the world of gardening. Find out more about the plants around you. Gardening is good for the **environment**. It's fun too!

It is easy to start. This book will give you simple tips. Learn about the plants you can grow. Get your hands dirty. Grow something great!

BUTTERFLY GARDENS

A butterfly garden is outdoors. You can plant your garden in the ground or use **containers**. Grow plants that **attract** butterflies. You can make a butterfly feeder too.

PLANT PLANNING

· · · · · · · · · · · · · · · · · · · ·

Butterfly gardens need planning to thrive! Learn about the butterflies that live in your area. Find out how to take care of the plants they love.

OUTSIDE GARDENS

Learn about the plants you plan to use. Some outdoor plants need to be in a certain type of area in order to grow.

Butterflies are summer insects. **Attract** them to your garden. Try planting red flowers. Have food in your garden for the butterflies to eat.

TOOLS

These are some of the important gardening tools you will be using for the projects in this book.

containers & pots

garden gloves

rubber gloves

hand trowel

plants

soil

rocks

watering can

SAFETY

Be safe and responsible while gardening. There are a few rules for doing gardening projects.

Ask Permission

Get **permission** to do a project. You might want to use tools or things around the house. Ask first!

Be Safe

Get help from an adult when using sharp tools or moving something heavy.

Clean Up

Clean up your working area when you are finished. Put everything away.

DIG INTO DIRT

· · · · · · · · · · · · · · · · · ·

Soil is the key to a healthy butterfly garden. The right kind of soil will help your plants grow best.

Choose the best soil for your plants. If you don't know, ask a gardener for help.

All-Purpose Garden Soil

This soil works best with outdoor plants. Buy soil with **peat moss** and **vermiculite**.

All-Purpose Potting Mix

This soil works well with most plants in pots. Buy soil with peat moss and vermiculite.

PLANT CARE

Water Watch

Remember to water your plants. Keep the soil moist. Watered plants will make more flowers for your butterflies.

Super Sunlight

Sunlight is important for flowers! Make sure they get the right light. Check how many hours of sunlight your plants need.

LOCATION STATION

Find a Spot
Butterflies like to eat in the sun. Plant your butterfly garden in an area that gets morning and afternoon sunlight.

Ground or Pot?
Planting a bigger garden in the ground will **attract** more butterflies. But a butterfly garden in pots will take up less space. Figure out which works best for your home.

Use the Right Size Pot

Plants need room to grow! The roots should not touch the sides of the pot.

TIP

Some pots have holes in the bottom. This helps drain extra water. They should be placed on **saucers** to catch the water.

Small Pots

Pots less than 8 inches (20 cm) deep.

Medium Pots

Pots 8 inches (20 cm) to 16 inches (40.5 cm) deep.

Large Pots

Pots deeper than 16 inches (40.5 cm).

BUTTERFLY NECESSITIES

Water

Butterflies get thirsty! See how to make a butterfly bar on page 16.

Food

Butterflies love sweet foods. Learn how to make a butterfly feeder on page 20.

BUTTERFLY FAVORITES

Butterflies are **attracted** to plants that have a lot of nectar. Here are some nectar-rich plants.

Aster	Hollyhock	Phlox
Bee balm	Lavender	Privet
Butterfly bush	Lilac	Rock cress
Catmint	Lupine	Sage
Cornflower	Mallow	Sea holly
Daylily	Milkweed	Snapdragon
Globe thistle	Mint	Sweet alyssum
Goldenrod	Pansy	Zinnia

BUTTERFLY BAR

GIVE BUTTERFLIES A PLACE TO DRINK!

Supplies

newspaper

5-inch (13 cm)
terra-cotta saucer

8-inch (20 cm)
terra-cotta saucer

4-inch (10 cm)
terra-cotta pot

3-inch (7.6 cm)
terra-cotta pot

sealant spray

acrylic paint

foam brush

paintbrush

heavy-duty glue

sand

rocks

watering can

DIRECTIONS

1. Cover your work area with newspaper. Place the pots and **saucers** on the newspaper. Have an adult spray all the pots and the saucers with sealant. Follow the directions on the sealant **container**.

2. Paint both of the saucers red. Let them dry. Add more coats if needed.

3. Paint the large pot blue. Let it dry. Add more coats if needed.

4. Paint the small pot orange. Let it dry. Add more coats if needed.

Project continues on the next page

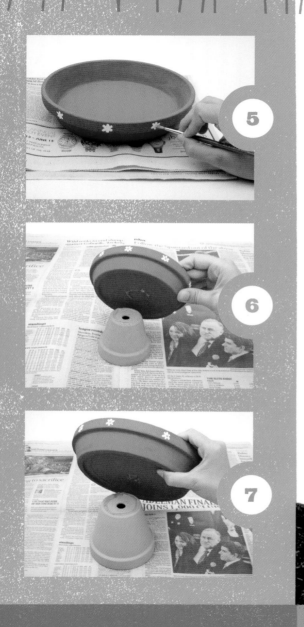

5 Paint flowers or other **designs** on the **saucers**. Let the paint dry.

6 Glue the bottom of the small saucer to the bottom of the orange pot. Let the glue dry.

7 Glue the bottom of the large saucer to the bottom of the blue pot. Let the glue dry.

8 Glue the rim of the orange pot in the center of the large **saucer**. Let the glue dry.

9 Fill the saucers halfway with sand. Add rocks for the butterflies to land on.

10 Add water to the saucers. Fill them until the sand is covered. Put the butterfly bar in your garden.

FUN FEEDER

A SWEET TREAT FOR BUTTERFLIES!

Supplies

• • • • • • • • •

newspaper

heavy-duty glue

4-inch (10 cm)
terra-cotta pot

6-inch (15 cm)
terra-cotta saucer

flat-backed glass tiles,
various shapes & colors

rubber gloves

outdoor tile grout

bucket

paint stir stick

sponge

paper towels

sealant spray

scissors

sugar

measuring cup

DIRECTIONS

1 Cover your work area with newspaper.

2 Put glue on the bottom of the pot. Glue the pot to the bottom of the **saucer**. Let the glue dry.

3 Glue glass tiles to the outside of the pot. Let it dry at least 4 hours.

4 Turn the pot and saucer over. Glue glass tiles to the inside of the saucer. Let it dry at least 4 hours.

Project continues on the next page

5 Put on rubber gloves. Have an adult help mix about 1 pound (.5 kg) of tile grout. Follow the directions on the package.

6 Put grout on the pot and **saucer**. Fill all the spaces between the tiles.

7 Let the grout dry 10 minutes. Wipe the pot and saucer with a moist sponge. Clean the grout off of the glass tiles.

8 Let the feeder dry 24 hours. Wipe the feeder with paper towels.

9 Have an adult spray the feeder with sealant. Let it dry 24 hours.

10 Mix ½ cup hot water and ¼ cup sugar together. Heat the mixture in the microwave 30 seconds. Keep heating and stirring it until the sugar **dissolves**. Pour the mixture into the **saucer**. Put the feeder in your garden.

COOL CARE Wash out your butterfly feeder once a week. Use warm water. It keeps the butterflies healthy!

GARDEN IN A BAG

MAKE YOUR GARDEN COME ALIVE!

OUTSIDE DIRECT SUN

Supplies

. . . .

1 40-pound (18 kg) bag of potting soil

scissors

ruler

garden gloves

hand trowel

2 zinnia seedlings

1 starflower seedling

1 joe-pye weed

1 butterfly bush seedling

2 petunia seedlings

2 milkweed seedlings

2 marigold seedlings

1 red fountain grass plant

4 impatiens plants

watering can

DIRECTIONS

1. Cut four slits on one side of the bag of soil. Make them about 5 inches (12.7 cm) long. Turn the bag over. Cut a large "x" in the side of the bag.

2. Peel back the plastic. Tuck each of the corners under the bag.

3. Dig a long, narrow hole in the soil near one side of the bag.

4. Take the zinnia seedlings, the starflower seedling, the joe-pye weed, and the butterfly bush seedling out of their trays. Pull gently at the roots to loosen them. Place the plants in the hole.

Project continues on the next page

5 Add soil around the plants. Cover the roots. Press the soil firmly.

6 Dig a second long hole about 1 inch (2 cm) in front of the first one.

7 Repeat steps 4 and 5 with the petunia and milkweed seedlings and 1 marigold seedling.

8 Dig a third long hole about 1 inch (2 cm) in front of the second one.

9. Repeat steps 4 and 5 with the second marigold seedling and the fountain grass.

10. Dig a fourth long hole about 1 inch (2 cm) in front of the third one.

11. Repeat steps 4 and 5 with the impatiens.

12. Place the bag outside in a sunny area. Water the plants.

COOL CARE

Water the plants every few days in the summer. Prune the leaves and flowers if the plants become too big.

BOOT PLANTER

BRING BUTTERFLIES TO YOUR GARDEN!

CAUTION SHARP!

OUTSIDE DIRECT SUN

Supplies

• • • • • • • •

newspaper

rain boots

acrylic paint

paintbrush

Mod Podge

foam brush

craft knife

potting soil

garden gloves

hand trowel

4 red zinnia
seedlings

watering can

fertilizer

DIRECTIONS

1 Cover your work area with newspaper.

2 Paint flowers or other **designs** on the rain boots. Let the paint dry.

3 Cover the boots with Mod Podge. Let it dry.

4 Have an adult cut a hole in the back of each boot.

Project continues on the next page

5 Cut a hole in each side of the toe of each boot.

6 Fill each boot with potting soil. Stop filling the boots 5 inches (13 cm) from the top.

7 Take the zinnias out of their trays. Pull gently on the roots to loosen them.

8 Put 2 zinnia plants in each boot.

9 Add more soil to the boots. Cover the roots. Press the soil firmly around the plants.

10 Water the zinnias well. Place the boots outside. Put them in a spot with a lot of sun.

COOL CARE Water the zinnias twice a week. Add **fertilizer** once every two weeks.

GLOSSARY

attract – to cause someone or something to come near.

container – something that other things can be put into.

design – a decorative pattern or arrangement.

dissolve – to mix with a liquid so that it becomes part of the liquid.

environment – nature and everything in it, such as the land, sea, and air.

fertilizer – something used to make plants grow better in soil.

peat moss – a type of moss that usually grows on wet land and is used in gardening.

permission – when a person in charge says it's okay to do something.

saucer – a shallow dish that goes under something to catch spills.

vermiculite – a light material that holds water that is often added to potting soil.